DATE DUE

Dylan & Cole Sprouse

Katie Franks

PowerKiDS press™

New York

Published in 2009 by The Rosen Publishing Group, Inc.
29 East 21st Street, New York, NY 10010

First Edition

Editor: Nicole Pristash
Book Design: Kate Laczynski
Photo Researcher: Jessica Gerweck

Photo Credits: Cover, pp. 1, 4, 8, 12 ,16, 19, 20 © Getty Images, Inc.; p. 7 © Ron Galella, Ltd./Getty Images; p. 11 © Arnaldo Magnani/Getty Images; p. 15 © Amy Graves/Getty Images.

Library of Congress Cataloging-in-Publication Data

Franks, Katie.
  Dylan and Cole Sprouse / by Katie Franks. — 1st ed.
      p. cm. — (Kid stars!)
  Includes index.
  ISBN 978-1-4042-4464-1 (library binding) ISBN 978-1-4042-4529-7 (pbk)
  ISBN 978-1-4042-4547-1 (6-pack)
  1. Sprouse, Dylan, 1992– —Juvenile literature. 2. Sprouse, Cole, 1992– —Juvenile literature. 3. Actors—United States—Biography—Juvenile literature. I. Title.
  PN2287.S6646F73 2009
  791.4302'8092s—dc22
  [B]
                                      2007049958

Manufactured in the United States of America

Contents

Even though they are twins, Dylan (left) and Cole (right) are very different from one another. Dylan is quieter while Cole is more talkative!

Meet the Sprouse Brothers

Dylan and Cole Sprouse are the stars of the TV show *The Suite Life of Zack & Cody*. They are also **twin** brothers. Look closely and you can tell which one is which. Cole has a mole on the left side of his chin, and Dylan has more freckles.

Dylan and Cole have been working together since they were babies, appearing in both TV shows and movies. These two talented stars have many fans all over the world. Here's a look at what Dylan and Cole have done and what they hope to do in the **future**!

California Boys

Dylan and Cole were born on August 4, 1992. Their mother and father gave the boys special names. Dylan was named after Dylan Thomas, a Welsh writer. Cole was named after the **jazz musician** Nat King Cole.

The boys were born in Arezzo, Italy. Their mom and dad taught English there. Shortly after the boys were born, the family moved back to the United States, to southern California. When they were six months old, the boys' grandmother suggested that Dylan and Cole start acting. They have been doing so ever since.

Dylan (left) is 15 minutes older than Cole (right). Cole says his brother often uses that fact to try to boss him around!

Cole (left) and Dylan (right) are just like other brothers and sisters. They sometimes fight over little things, but they always make up.

An Early Start

Dylan and Cole began acting in **commercials** when they were babies. They often played the same role, or part. Being twins helped the boys get these roles. This is because a child can work only for a short time each day on a TV show or movie. By using twins, a crew can work twice as long as they can with one child.

Dylan and Cole's first big job came before they could even walk! In 1993, they won a shared part on the TV show *Grace Under Fire*, playing the baby, Patrick Kelley. The show lasted five years.

Movie Time

After *Grace Under Fire* ended, Dylan and Cole got even bigger parts. In 1999, when they were seven, the boys landed a part in the movie *Big Daddy,* with Adam Sandler. They played a character named Julian, a boy who gets to do whatever he wants. This meant the boys got to wear weird clothes and have a lot of fun!

As they got older, the boys wanted roles of their own. In 2000, Cole began playing the character Ben on the TV show *Friends*. Both boys like playing different parts because when they shared roles, they saw less of each other.

Adam Sandler (right) thought Cole (left) and Dylan were very talented. He did not mind that they got all the attention in *Big Daddy*!

11

In 2005, Cole (left), Brenda Song (middle), and Dylan (right) hosted Kid's Day in Hollywood, California. Brenda plays London Tipton on *The Suite Life*.

The Suite Life of Zack & Cody

Dylan and Cole's big break came in 2005. The boys got their own show on Disney, called *The Suite Life of Zack & Cody*. They play twin brothers, Zack and Cody Martin. Their characters live in a **suite** in a **hotel**, where their mother works as a singer.

Zack, played by Dylan, likes girls and skateboarding, but he does not like school. Cody, played by Cole, is very different. Cody likes to study and to cook. He plays along with Zack's wild ideas and tries to keep Zack out of trouble. It does not always work, though!

The Life of Dylan and Cole

The Suite Life of Zack & Cody quickly became one of Disney's most **popular** shows. Dylan and Cole began appearing in teen magazines and on other TV shows. Kids everywhere started to know who they were. Girls saw the brothers as heartthrobs, or cute boys they wanted to know more about. The boys were suddenly even more famous. Dylan has said that sudden fame has been a bit scary but **exciting**.

Because Dylan and Cole spend so much time working together, you might think they do everything together. Both boys, however, have interests that make them different.

The Sprouse brothers use their fame for good causes. Here they are seen reading at a Halloween carnival that was raising money for sick children.

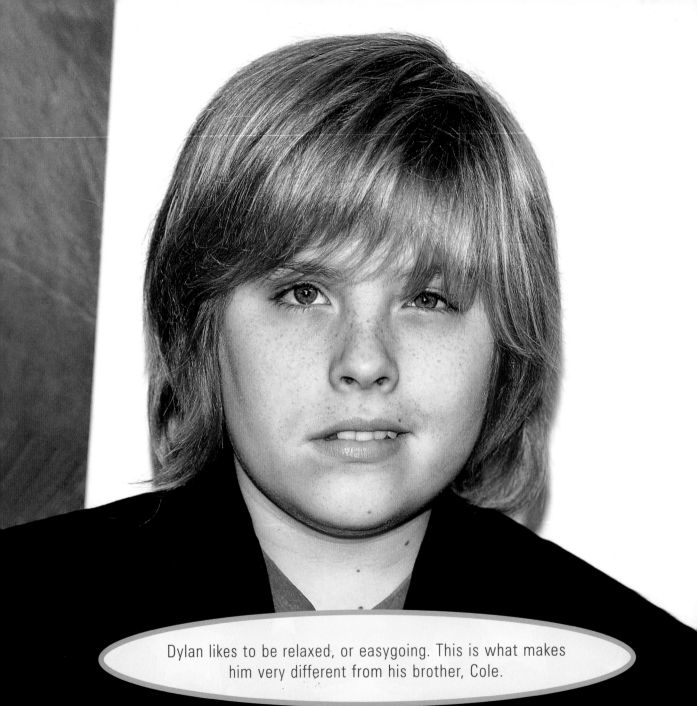

Dylan likes to be relaxed, or easygoing. This is what makes him very different from his brother, Cole.

Dylan

Dylan is a little bit like his character, Zack, on *The Suite Life of Zack & Cody*. He likes to play jokes on Cole and is more into sports than his brother. Like a true California kid, Dylan likes skateboarding and snowboarding. He also likes reading **comic books** and playing video games.

Dylan thinks it is cool to be a twin. He has said that even though he and Cole sometimes fight, they always look out for each other. He views Cole as his best friend even though they can be very different at times.

Cole

Like Dylan, Cole is a little like his *Suite Life* character, Cody. Both Cole and his character like school, mostly math class. Cole writes in a journal every day, too. He likes writing in it so much that he talked Dylan into starting a journal as well. Cole also likes playing rock music on his guitar.

Cole has also said that it is great to be a twin, even though Dylan sometimes tries to boss him around. Cole says that when you have a twin, you never feel lonely and almost always have someone to talk to.

Cole likes to keep busy at all times. Because of this, Dylan says Cole is a lot of fun to be around.

Dylan (left) and Cole (right) showed their clothing line at the Camp Ronald McDonald Celebrity Teen Fashion Show on May 5, 2007, in Los Angeles, California.

What's Next?

The third season of *The Suite Life of Zack & Cody* started in 2007. What else are the boys up to?

The brothers set up their own brand, called D.C. Sprouse. The boys will use this brand to make video games, CDs, DVDs, and other things that teens will like. The boys even have their own clothing line. They also started a book **series**, called 47 R.O.N.I.N. The books are about twin brothers who go on **adventures**. Dylan and Cole hope that these **projects** and their work in the future will help them go from kid stars to superstars!

DYLAN

COLE

 Dylan is 5 feet 3 ½ inches (1.61 m) tall.

 Cole is 5 feet 4 inches (1.63 m) tall.

 Dylan's **favorite** class in school is science.

 Cole's favorite class in school is math.

 One of Dylan's nicknames is Lumpkin.

 One of Cole's nicknames is Coley Moley.

 Dylan likes to draw and to read comic books.

 Cole likes to play the guitar.

 Dylan and Cole have been snowboarding since they were four years old.

 The brothers are big fans of the L.A. Lakers basketball team.

Glossary

adventures (ed-VEN-cherz) Fun things to do.

comic books (KO-mik BUHKS) Booklets with stories told in cartoons.

commercials (kuh-MER-shulz) TV or radio messages trying to sell something.

exciting (ik-SY-ting) Very interesting.

favorite (FAY-vuh-rut) Most liked.

future (FYOO-chur) The time that is coming.

hotel (ho-TEL) A place where you pay to stay overnight.

jazz (JAZ) A lively type of music.

musician (myoo-ZIH-shun) A person who writes, plays, or sings music.

popular (PAH-pyuh-lur) Liked by lots of people.

projects (PRAH-jekts) Plans to do something.

series (SIR-eez) A group of things that come one after another that are alike.

suite (SWEET) A group of hotel rooms that is set up like an apartment.

twin (TWIN) One of a pair that is exactly the same.

Index

Web Sites

Due to the changing nature of Internet links, PowerKids Press has developed an online list of Web sites related to the subject of this book. This site is updated regularly. Please use this link to access the list:
www.powerkidslinks.com/kids/sprouse/